Ancient Egypt

Jinny Johnson

KINGFISHER

First published 2013 by Kingfisher
an imprint of Macmillan Children's Books
a division of Macmillan Publishers Limited
20 New Wharf Road, London N1 9RR
Basingstoke and Oxford
Associated companies throughout the world
www.panmacmillan.com

Consultant: Dr Joann Fletcher, University of York

Illustrations by: Peter Bull Art Studio

ISBN 978-0-7534-3264-8

Copyright © Macmillan Children's Books 2013

All rights reserved. No part of this publication may be
reproduced, stored in or introduced into a retrieval system,
or transmitted, in any form or by any means (electronic,
mechanical, photocopying, recording or otherwise), without
the prior written permission of the publisher. Any person who
does any unauthorized act in relation to this publication may
be liable to criminal prosecution and civil claims for damages.

1 3 5 7 9 8 6 4 2
1TR/0912/UTD/WKT/140MA

A CIP catalogue record for this book is available from
the British Library.

Printed in China

This book is sold subject to the condition that it shall not,
by way of trade or otherwise, be lent, resold, hired out,
or otherwise circulated without the publisher's prior consent
in any form of binding or cover other than that in which it
is published and without a similar condition including this
condition being imposed on the subsequent purchaser.

Picture credits

The Publisher would like to thank the following
for permission to reproduce their material.
Every care has been taken to trace copyright
holders. However, if there have been unintentional
omissions or failure to trace copyright holders,
we apologise and will, if informed, endeavour
to make corrections in any future edition.
(t = top, b = bottom, c = centre, l = left, r = right):

Pages 4l Getty/Hulton; 4br Getty/Bridgeman; 5tl Corbis/Charles & Josette
Lenars; 5tc Shutterstock/Arthur R; 5tr AKG/De Agostini Picture Library;
5cr AKG/George Ortitz Collection; 5bl AKG/IAM/World History Archive;
5br AKG/De Agostini Picture Library; 6tl Shutterstock/Timothy Craig
Lubcke; 8l NASA; 8cr Shutterstock/Doctor Jools; 8br Shutterstock/
BasPhoto; 9tl With the very kind permission of the trustees of the British
Museum (BM); 9tr Art Archive/Dagli Orti; 9cl BM; 9br BM; 10bl Corbis/
Sandro Vannini; 12r BM; 12b BM; 13tl Bridgeman Art Library (BAL)/Fitzwilliam
Museum, Cambridge; 13tr AKG/ De Agostini Picture Library; 13cl BM;
13cr Corbis/Sandro Vannini; 13br Corbis/Sandro Vannini; 14bl Art Archive/
Dagli Orti; 16l AKG/ Rijksmuseum van Oudheden; 16r Corbis/Jean-Pierre
Lescourret; 17tl Corbis/ Michael Nicholson; 17tr AKG/Gerard Degeorge;
17cr AKG/ Herve Champollion; 17b Corbis; 18tl Corbis/ Sandro Vannini;
20l AKG/Ullstein Bild Archiv; 20r Corbis/Sandro Vannini; 20–21 AKG/ Museo
Egizio; 21tl AA/Dagli Orti; 21cr AKG/ Gerard Degeorge; 21br Corbis/Gianni
Dagli Orti; 22bl BM; 24c Art Archive/Dagli Orti; 24r BM; 24b BM; 25tr BM;
25cl BM; 25cr BM; 25b Corbis/Sandro Vannini; 26bl Alamy/Prisma Archivo;
28tr Photolibrary/Imagebroker; 28bl Photolibrary /JD Dallet; 28br Corbis/
Gianni Dagli Orti; 29tl Corbis/ Sandro Vannini; 29tr Art Archive/Dagli Orti;
29cr AKG/Egyptisches Museum; 29bl Getty/BAL; 29br AKG/Egyptian
Museum, Cairo; 30tl BM; 30tr BM; 30ctr Art Archive/Gianni Dagli Orti;
30cbl Shutterstock/Mariejie; 30bl BAL/Ashmolean Museum; 30br BAL/
Brooklyn Museum; 31ctr Art Archive/Alfredo Dagli Orti; 30cbl Shutterstock/
Christopher Tan Teck Haen; 31cbr Shutterstock/Mogens Tolle; 31br Art
Archive/Dagli Orti.

Contents

More to explore

On some of the pages in this book, you will find coloured buttons with symbols on them. There are four different colours, and each belongs to a different topic. Choose a topic, follow its coloured buttons through the book, and you'll make some interesting discoveries of your own.

For example, on page 7 you'll find a green button, like this, next to a hippo. The green buttons are about Egyptian animals.

Page 11

Animals

There is a page number in the button. Turn to that page (page 11) to find a green button next to a donkey. Follow all the steps through the book, and at the end of your journey you'll find out how the steps are linked, and discover even more information about this topic.

Gods and goddesses

Jobs

Everyday objects

The other topics in this book are gods and goddesses, jobs and everyday objects. Follow the steps and see what you can discover!

The ancient Egyptian world

Ancient Egyptians lived thousands of years ago, but they ate, worked and cared for their families, just like we do. We know lots about how they lived from the many amazing paintings, buildings and objects they left behind.

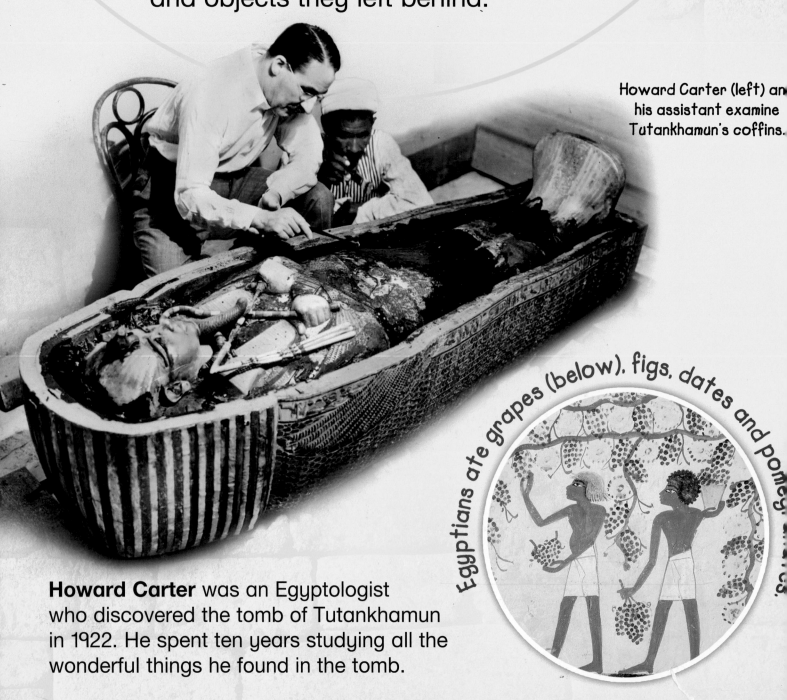

Howard Carter (left) and his assistant examine Tutankhamun's coffins.

Egyptians ate grapes (below), figs, dates and pomegranates.

Howard Carter was an Egyptologist who discovered the tomb of Tutankhamun in 1922. He spent ten years studying all the wonderful things he found in the tomb.

In the **Predynastic Period** (c. 5500 to 3100BCE) people began to settle by the River Nile to grow crops and raise cattle.

a flint knife with an ivory handle from c. 3100BCE

The Egyptians took great care with their **appearance**. Many people shaved their heads and many wore wigs made from human hair.

The **Old Kingdom** (c. 3100 to 2181BCE) was the age of pyramid building. The Giza pyramids and Great Sphinx were made at this time.

the Step Pyramid at Saqqara – the world's earliest large stone building

Middle Kingdom rulers (2055 to 1650BCE) improved trade in Egypt. Art and literature flourished too.

a jewelled falcon from the tomb of Tutankhamun, a New Kingdom pharaoh

The **New Kingdom** (1550 to 1069BCE) was a time of great wealth and success in Egypt, when the empire was at its largest.

Amenemhat III was a Middle Kingdom pharaoh.

Cleopatra VII ruled Egypt after the end of the Late Period.

In the **Late Period** (747 to 332BCE) Egypt was ruled by the Persians. Alexander the Great ruled the country from 332 to 323BCE.

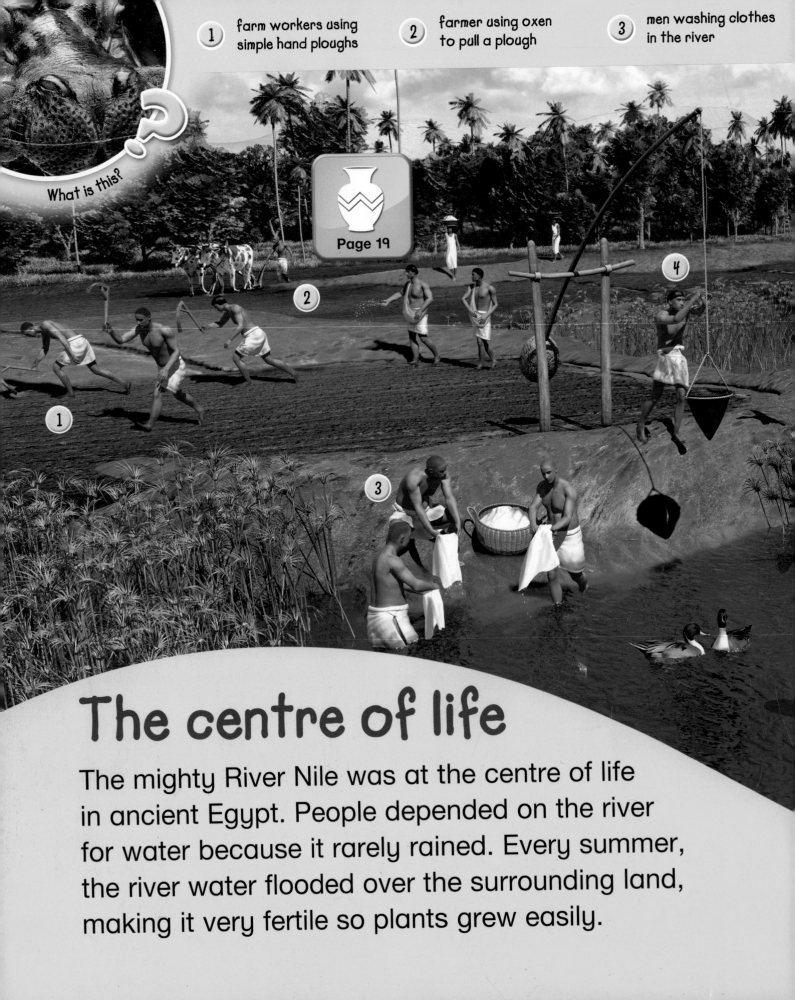

Page 19

What is this?

1 farm workers using simple hand ploughs

2 farmer using oxen to pull a plough

3 men washing clothes in the river

The centre of life

The mighty River Nile was at the centre of life in ancient Egypt. People depended on the river for water because it rarely rained. Every summer, the river water flooded over the surrounding land, making it very fertile so plants grew easily.

After the flood, people are busy working. By the river, farmers scatter seeds on the dark soil and tend animals. Food crops include grain for making bread and beer, as well as vegetables and fruit. On the river, fishermen in boats pull up nets full of fish. Fish was an important food for the ancient Egyptians.

Page 23

Page 11

6

5

This is a hippopotamus, one of the most dangerous animals in the Nile.

The great river highway

People depended on the River Nile for transport as well as water. It was hard to travel across the land, which was mostly desert. Goods and people moved by boat up and down the country.

Red Land (desert)

Red Land (desert)

The Nile is 6,741km long, the longest river in the world

Boats, such as these feluccas, are still important for travel in Egypt today.

The temple of Edfu on the Nile's west bank is dedicated to the god Horus.

The **rich soil** along the banks of the Nile where crops could be grown was called the 'Black Land'. Beyond that was the 'Red Land', the desert.

People hunted water birds on the Nile as well as fish. Can you see the hunter's cat attacking birds in this painting from the tomb of Nebamun?

This weight helped lift the bucket out of the river.

Boats were placed in tombs so that the dead could use them in the afterlife.

Farmers used a **shaduf** (a long pole with a bucket at one end and a weight at the other) to lift river water. The bucket was lowered into the water, then raised again using the weight.

The **flooding of the Nile** was so important it even had its own god, called Hapy. Here he is shown coloured blue and holding a palm leaf stem.

Boats were so important to life in ancient Egypt that models such as this one were often placed in tombs. This boat is made of wood and linen.

Daily life

Most ordinary people lived in simple houses with one or two rooms. The houses were built from mud bricks, which were made of mud and sometimes straw and dried in the sun. Small windows kept houses cool in summer and warm on cold nights.

In the house, a farmer finishes his first meal of the day, while his family bustle around with their work. There is a statue of a god and not much furniture – stools, a table and sleeping mats on the flat roof. Outside, the farmer's wife is grinding grain to make bread. She and the rest of the family wear clothes of rough linen.

What is this?

1 storage jars of food kept cool underground

2 cattle kept for work, meat and milk

3 flat roof used as a living and sleeping are

? This is a board game called senet, which was popular with the ancient Egyptians.

3

Page 15

4

5

Page 26

Page 15

6

(4) shrine for Bes, a household god

(5) outdoor oven for baking bread

(6) donkey used by a farmer to carry heavy loads

Egyptians at home

Ancient Egyptian homes were all made from mud bricks. Ordinary homes usually had only one storey and were simply decorated and furnished. Wealthy homes were larger with more furniture and colourful paintwork inside.

Bes was also one of the gods of magic.

Some wealthier homes had beautiful **gardens** with trees and water, where the family could relax. The home shown below belonged to a royal scribe and his family.

Bes, a **household god**, might look fierce, but in fact he was believed to protect the house from evil spirits.

Wealthy Egyptians wore fine linen clothes and precious jewels. Some men, women and even children wore black make-up called kohl around their eyes.

a monkey-shaped pot for storing kohl

This mirror is made from highly polished bronze.

This cat's mouth could be opened and shut by pulling a string.

Wealthy families had many **toys**, such as this little wooden cat, for their children to play with.

Servants gave floral necklaces and perfume to guests at a banquet.

dress made from fine linen

gold and turquoise bracelet

The pharaohs

The king or leader of ancient Egypt was called a pharaoh. The word pharaoh comes from the Egyptian 'per-aa', meaning palace. The pharaoh owned the land and ruled the people, and led troops into battle against Egypt's enemies.

Thutmose III was pharaoh from 1479 to 1425BCE, and he was a great warrior. He is said never to have lost a battle. Here he is leading a charge against rebels in a neighbouring land, ruled by the Egyptians. Thutmose rides in a splendid chariot, while his soldiers follow behind on foot, carrying weapons.

What is this?

1   horse with colourful headdress

2   war dogs, used for attack and defence

3   horse-drawn chario of fine gold

? This is the Blue Crown or war crown, which pharaohs often wore when going into battle.

Page 22

Page 19

Page 30

4 Pharaoh Thutmose III in battle dress

5 warriors with spears and bows and arrows

6 scribe ready to record the casualties of battle

Leaders of the kingdom

A pharaoh was seen as half-human, half-god, and represented the gods on Earth. The kingship usually passed from father to son, and one of a pharaoh's tasks was to make sure a tomb and temple were built for the previous ruler.

Hatshepsut was one of at least six women to be crowned king of Egypt. She ruled for almost 22 years during the New Kingdom era.

Nefertiti wearing her famous tall blue crown

hieroglyphs of the throne name (left) and birth name of Ramesses II, who ruled for 67 years

Pharaoh Merenptah (left) with the sun god Ra

Tutankhamun, shown here on his throne, became pharaoh when he was only about nine years old. He ruled for about ten years and died when he was 18 or 19 years old.

Pharaoh Akhenaten and Nefertiti, his wife and co-ruler, enjoy playtime with three of their daughters in this picture. They worshipped only Aten, a form of the sun god Ra.

rays of Aten, the sun disc

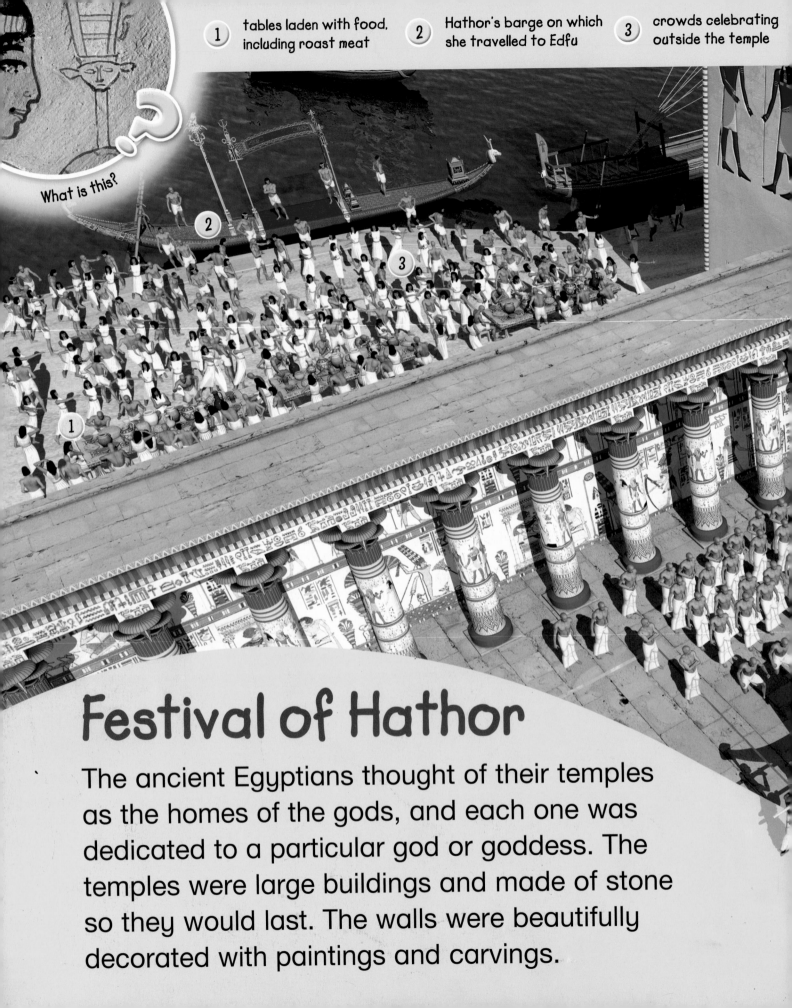

What is this?

1 tables laden with food, including roast meat

2 Hathor's barge on which she travelled to Edfu

3 crowds celebrating outside the temple

Festival of Hathor

The ancient Egyptians thought of their temples as the homes of the gods, and each one was dedicated to a particular god or goddess. The temples were large buildings and made of stone so they would last. The walls were beautifully decorated with paintings and carvings.

4 — boat-like shrines in which statues of gods are carried

5 — high priestess shaking her sistrum rattle

6 — dancers and musicians playing tambourines

19

Page 23

Page 11

It is the festival of the goddess Hathor, when her statue is brought up the Nile to visit the temple of Horus at Edfu for two weeks. As the statue is carried into the inner temple, people gather outside to cheer and celebrate. There is plenty of food and wine for the crowds, as well as music and entertainment.

This is a sistrum, a musical instrument that made a rattling sound and was usually played by women.

Gods and goddesses

The ancient Egyptians worshipped many gods and goddesses. Some were linked to vital elements in life such as the sun or the Nile flood. Others gave protection or represented places, plants or animals.

the sun god Ra with a sun disc above his head

Ra was the sun god so he was one of the most important. He is usually shown with a falcon's head, topped with a sun disc, and solar rays radiate from him.

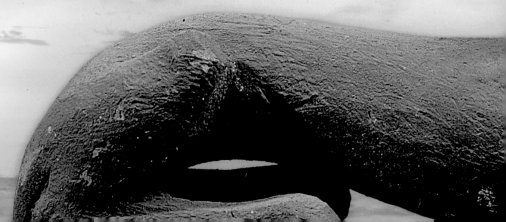

Amun was a very powerfu god. This statue of the go was made during the reig of Tutankhamun and shows the god with the pharaoh's features.

The gods **Horus** and Sobek and the goddess Isis were all protection gods. Horus (left) was the god of the sky and he also protected the pharaoh.

Sobek was a god of the Nile. He represented the might of the pharaoh.

Anubis was one of the gods of the dead and of the process of mummification. He was usually shown with a jackal's head or as a jackal, as in this wooden sculpture.

Isis was a very powerful goddess, known for her magic and her protection of the young.

Preparing a mummy

The Egyptians believed that if a person were to enjoy life after death – the afterlife – the body must be preserved as a home for the spirit (or soul). To do this, they treated and wrapped the body in a special way. This process was called mummification.

A priest says prayers and spells while embalmers wrap the body in linen strips brushed with resins and oils. Before this, the body was washed and the internal organs, except for the heart, were removed. Then it was dried out with a special salt called natron for 40 days, and packed with earth, linen or wood shavings.

Page 30

What is this?

2

1

1 canopic jars for storing the internal organs

2 painted wooden coffin for the body

3 perfumed oils and resins

? A scarab beetle amulet was placed in the mummy's wrappings to protect the person from harm.

Page 27

Page 30

4 strips of linen for wrapping the body

5 Amulets were placed between layers of linen.

6 priest wearing Anubis mask

Afterlife

After mummification, a ceremony called the Opening of the Mouth took place. The Egyptians believed this ritual opened the mouth, eyes, ears and nose so that the person's spirit inside the body could live in the afterlife.

The **Opening of the Mouth** was performed by a priest, with mourners and other priests. Food and drink were given so the dead person had food for the afterlife.

tools used for the Opening of the Mouth

The **coffin** covered the mummy when it was complete. The richer the person, the more elaborate and beautiful the coffin was.

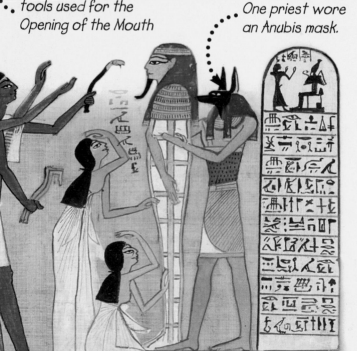

One priest wore an Anubis mask.

Shabtis were small figures that were placed in the tomb with the body. They represented servants who would work for the dead person in the afterlife.

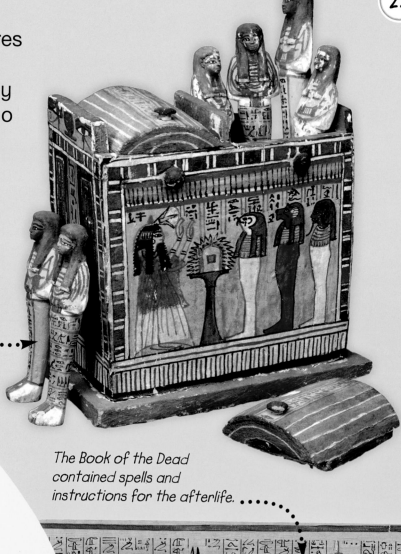

The shabti figures were believed to come to life.

The Book of the Dead contained spells and instructions for the afterlife.

a mummy being carried into the afterlife on a sacred Apis bull

Most **animal mummies** were of sacred animals linked to gods. They were made as offerings to the gods. Some people had their pets mummified, too.

crocodile mummy

Pyramids and tombs

The mighty pyramids were built as tombs for pharaohs. They were made of stone and had four triangular-shaped sides that met in a point at the top. Inside a pyramid was usually a maze of passages and burial chambers.

Page 30

What is this?

1 architects with papyrus plans

2 stone block being moved up a ramp

3 workers sharpening their tools

? The owl is one of four hieroglyphs in the ancient Egyptian word for 'pyramid'.

27

After years of work by thousands of men, the pyramid is nearly complete. Architects study building details, while a large group of workers struggle to pull a huge block of stone to the top of the pyramid. During the final stages, limestone blocks are added to make the smooth, gleaming-white surface of the pyramid.

Page 15

4 stoneworkers shaping blocks of stone

5 completed pyramid with its gold tip

6 using a tool to check the stone block is the right shape

Royal tombs

Not all pharaohs were buried in pyramids. Later rulers were buried in tombs cut into rock in an area called the Valley of the Kings. One of the most famous of these is the tomb of Tutankhamun.

Tombs in the Valley of the Kings were hidden in the rocks and so they were harder for tomb raiders to find. Pyramids were often robbed of their treasures.

The tomb of Sety I was the largest of the king's tombs. It is also the most beautiful in the Valley of the Kings, as shown by this wall painting from inside the tomb.

Horemheb, as shown in a painting in his tomb in the Valley of the Kings

This **death mask** was found on Tutankhamun's mummy in his tomb. It is made from gold and lapis lazuli and decorated with precious stones.

This piece of jewellery made from gold and precious stones was found in the wrappings of Tutankhamun's mummy.

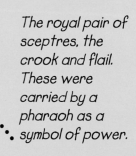

The royal pair of sceptres, the crook and flail. These were carried by a pharaoh as a symbol of power.

Tutankhamun was not the greatest pharaoh, but his treasures such as these have made him famous. His tomb had hundreds of precious objects for the afterlife.

a statue of the goddess Selket, who guarded the pharaoh's internal organs

Nefertari, one of the many wives of Ramesses II

Nefertari plays senet in this painting from her tomb.

Everyday objects

Egyptian farmers used hand ploughs as well as **ploughs pulled by cattle** to break up the soil before sowing crops. Ploughs were made of wood.

The **sistrum**, a bronze rattle, was one of many musical instruments played by the ancient Egyptians. Music and dance were both important parts of festivals.

chief embalmer

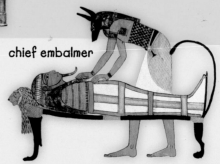

Jobs

fishing boat

Plenty of fish swim in the Nile. They were caught by **fishermen** for people to eat at home and to feed the workers on tombs and pyramids. They used harpoons as well as nets and lines.

Embalmers carried out the mummification process on a body. They used many special substances to help dry out and preserve the dead.

Animals

The **hippopotamus** was the largest animal in the Nile. It was both feared and worshipped. Tawaret, the goddess of childbirth, was often shown with a hippo's head and body.

Donkeys were used to carry loads and to help with threshing. They were led in circles over the grain to help separate the edible ears from the inedible chaff.

Gods and goddesses

Bastet was a protective goddess and household god, usually shown as a cat or with the head of a cat. She was a daughter of the sun god Ra.

Montu was the god of war, usually shown with a falcon's head and a headdress made up of a sun disc and two feathers. He was also associated with a type of bull, called the Buchis bull.

More to explore

Bread was the Egyptians' most important food. The grains of wheat were ground between two **stones** and the bread was baked in a wood-fired oven made from clay.

Papyrus was a paper-like material made from the stems of the papyrus plant, which grew around the River Nile. The stems were also used to make other items, such as baskets.

papyrus with the hieroglyphs for the word 'pyramid'

killed **stoneworkers** were eeded to build pyramids and ombs. They had to cut and hape large blocks of stone, uch as limestone, sandstone r granite.

cutting a block of stone

Scribes were among the few people in ancient Egypt who could read and write. They kept the official records for the pharaoh and his government, and wrote hieroglyphs for tombs and temples.

The **falcon**, a bird of prey, was sacred to the ancient Egyptians. The god Horus was usually shown with a falcon's head and the bird was also sacred to Montu, the god of war.

The **jackal** is a kind of wild dog. It was sacred to the ancient Egyptians and linked with the god Anubis. The canopic jar with a jackal's-head design held the stomach.

orus was one of the ost important gods nd was believed to e the protector of e pharaoh. He as often shown ith the head of a alcon and wearing red and white crown.

Anubis was the god of embalming and of the dead. He was shown as a jackal or with a jackal's head and priests often wore an Anubis mask during mummification ceremonies.

Index